Collins

SMART TECH

1

Manasi Kashikar
Sneha Krishnan

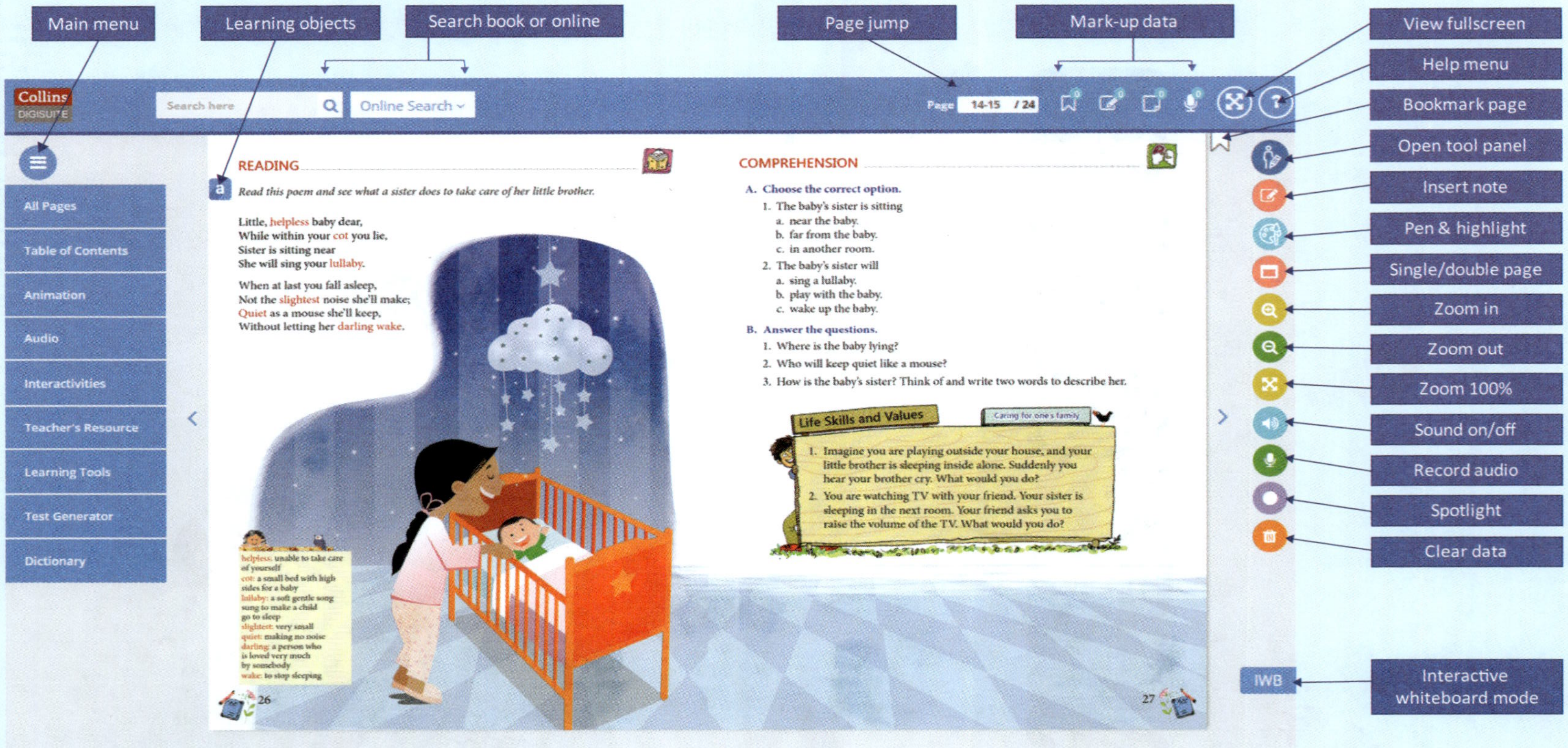

Student + Teacher

a animations

ilt instructor-led tutorials

ia activities

w worksheets

audio

g games

v videos

Teacher-only

lp lesson plans

w worksheets

tn teacher's notes

ak answer keys

PREFACE

Over the last few decades, technology has surrounded almost all aspects of our lives. It is remarkable that the pace at which technology evolves has also accelerated. In India, smartphones and the internet have become widely accessible, putting the power of technology in the hands of millions.

In this backdrop, we believe that it is important for students to:

- understand that technology is going to keep evolving, and it is a life skill to learn.
- know the basics of coding, which makes devices come to life. Coding skills are as essential today as basic Math and Language skills.
- take control of regulating their usage and make constructive use of their access to computer devices.

The ***Collins Smart Tech*** series adheres to the vision of the National Education Policy 2020. Through the series, we endeavour to acquaint students with technology in a way that is relatable, engaging and fun. Using Windows 10 and MS Office 2016, students are introduced to widely used tools. The series introduces computational thinking from class 2 onwards with the intent of developing the necessary skills that students need to acquire coding skills. The chapters on coding skills help students understand the logic behind the code and develop their own problem-solving and critical thinking abilities. The focus is on developing critical thinking and inquiry and enabling discovery-, discussion- and analysis-based teaching and learning methods for holistic education.

Now, children have exposure to computer devices and the internet from a young age. Basis our experience at MindChamp, students need to understand concepts in their context and not in an isolated fashion. Therefore, we have attempted to provide real-life instances that they can easily relate with as much as possible. Even topics such as AI, VR, AR and IoT have been covered with, the same zeal. This stands true for the theoretical as well as the practical aspects of the chapters. It is our sincere hope that teachers find imparting knowledge from this series as exciting as students learning from it.

Finally, we aspire to set a precedent for high-quality Computer Science education across the country that keeps up with the changes in technology. Observations, experiences, suggestions and critique from teachers and students alike act as our guide in carrying forward this aspiration.

We would like to thank our interns Janita George, Nisha Gokhale and Srinath K Nallamalli in helping us shape the content.

Key Features

What will I learn?
Outlines well-defined learning objectives in the form of questions that describe what students will learn in the chapter

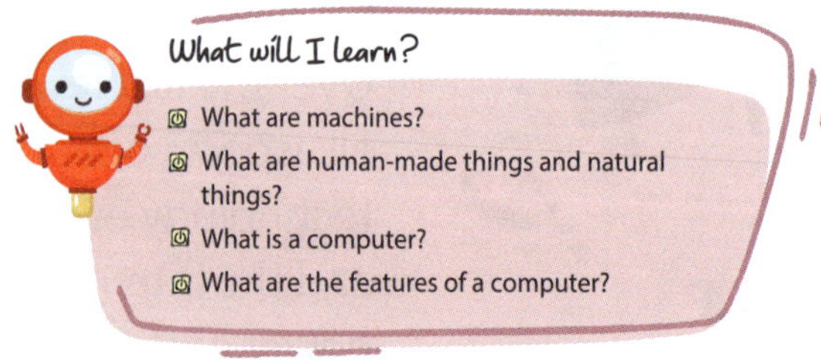

Think and Discuss
Includes various activities and real-life examples to set the context for what students are about to learn

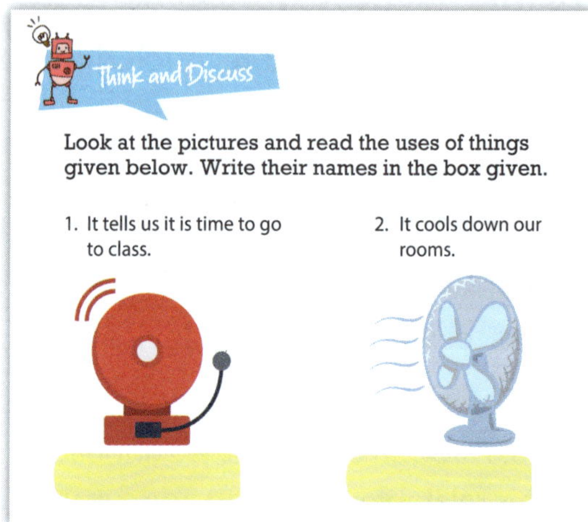

Knowledge Bytes
Contains additional information/facts about the topic being taught

Meaning
Gives contextual meaning of difficult words

I am smart!
Provides tips and shortcut tricks for the topics covered in the chapter to foster inquiry- and discovery-based learning

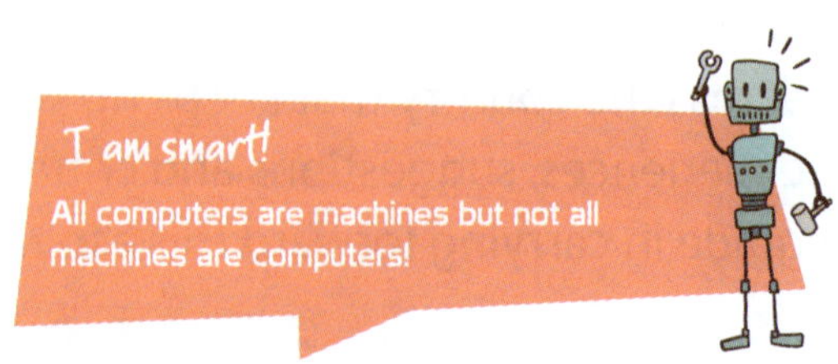

I can do!

Includes hands-on tasks for revision, based on the desired learning outcomes

> **I can do!**
>
> The up and down arrows appear with the Text tool.
> Click on them and find out what happens. Write down what you see.
>
> ....

I can tell!

Comprises short questions to reinforce the concept learnt and promote competency based education

> **I can tell!**
>
> Look at the keyboard carefully. Why is it called QWERTY keyboard?
> **Hint**: Check the third row on your keyboard.

What did I learn?

Revisits all the important points learnt in the chapter

> **What did I learn?**
>
> - Machines are human-made things. They perform many tasks easily and quickly.
> - A computer is a machine that helps us do many things.
> - A computer is a device that takes instructions from the user, stores and processes it and shows the result.

Exercises

Includes exhaustive revision exercises comprising a blend of both objective-type and detailed-answer type questions. Questions based on programming teach how to use and integrate technology in everyday life.

> **Exercises**
>
> 1. State whether the following statements are true (T) or false (F).
>
>   a. Mouse has a long wire connected to the CPU box. ☐

Lab Activity

Tests the practical application of the concepts taught to enhance comprehension and provide opportunities for peer tutoring

> **Lab Activity**
>
> Visit the Computer Lab. Do you see any smart machines there? Count and write the number of smart machines you see.

Worksheets

Comprises additional practice questions and projects to cater to traditional examination requirements

> **Worksheet 1**
>
> 1. Tick (✓) the correct answer.
>
>   a. Tick the part of the computer that is used to point on the screen.
>
>   (i) ☐ (ii) ☐ (iii) ☐

Skills section

Focused on a specific skill at each level, this section helps children acquire a skill that will be of use to them in the real world. Also includes hands-on projects to reinforce learning and facilitate cooperation

> **COMPUTER MANNERS**
>
> Always follow the instructions of your computer teacher in the lab.
>
> | 1. Do not pull or push the keyboard too hard. It may damage the wires. | 2. Do not use a wet cloth to clean the computer. It may damage its parts. |
> |---|---|

Contents

1 Computers Around Us

What will I learn?

- What are machines?
- What are human-made things and natural things?
- What is a computer?
- What are the features of a computer?

Think and Discuss

Look at the pictures and read the uses of things given below. Write their names in the box given.

1. It tells us it is time to go to class.

2. It cools down our rooms.

3. We play on it with our friend.

4. It keeps our things safe.

5. It helps us talk to people in far-off places.

6. It takes us from one place to another.

MACHINES—OLD AND NEW

A long time ago, we used to only grow food. We did not have any tools to help us. Even simple tasks took a lot of time and efforts. Then, we learned to make tools to make our tasks easy. For example, the wheel allowed us to make different means of transport. Today, be it cars or bicycles, wheels are used in many modes of transport. Figure 1.2 shows how wheels have been used in different modes of transport.

Fig. 1.1 *The first wheel*

Fig. 1.2 *Many uses of wheels*

There were many more inventions that helped reduce human efforts and perform many tasks easily. We named them **machines**!

A set of parts, which work together to perform a task and reduce human efforts make a machine.

A clock helps us to be on time. But, is it a machine? Do you know what each part of the clock does?

Part	What it does?	What they do together?
Hour hand	Points to the hour of the day.	
Minute hand	Points to the minute of the hour.	Show us the time!
Battery	Gives power to the hands.	

Fig. 1.3 *A clock*

HUMAN-MADE THINGS AND NATURAL THINGS

The things made by humans are called human-made things. Machines, clothes, books, etc. are made by humans. The things already present in nature are called natural things. Animals, trees, rivers, etc. are examples of natural things.

I can tell!

Look at the following pictures. Write 'H' for the human-made things and 'N' for the natural things, in the given box.

1.

2.

3.

4.

5.

6.

Machines make our life easy and comfortable. But is there a machine to help us think? Which machine do we use if we have to

- do Maths homework?
- add and subtract numbers?
- search information about anything in the world?
- draw a picture and save it?

A computer can do all these things.

ENTER THE WORLD OF COMPUTERS!

Look around you. Computers are very common and are used almost everywhere.

- Schools use computers to store information about their students, teachers and exam timetables.
- Railway stations and airports use computer to track all trains and aeroplanes.
- At home, computers are used to play games, listen to music, watch movies and search for information.

Fig. 1.4 *A computer system*

A computer is a smart machine used to perform tasks that require thinking power. It needs electricity to run.

Just like chocolates, computers are also made by different companies. Write down the names of three companies that make computers.

....

....

Features of a Computer

A computer has a lot of features, which make it a smart machine.

> A computer is a device that takes instructions from the user, stores and processes them, and shows the result.

- A computer is very fast.

- A computer is always correct.

- A computer can store a lot of information.

- A computer never gets tired.

- A computer never forgets anything.

- A computer can do many things at the same time.

- A computer has no emotions and feelings.
- A computer always follows the instructions given by the user.

I can tell!

Write down the features of a computer that are not present in a calculator.

....

....

....

....

What did I learn?

- Machines are human-made things. They perform many tasks easily and quickly.
- A computer is a machine that helps us do many things.
- A computer is a device that takes instructions from the user, stores and processes them and shows the result.
- A computer has a lot of features that make it a smart machine.

Exercises

1. Match the following.

a. 

b. 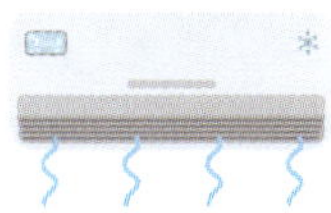

c. 

d. 

e. 

(i) It takes us from one place to another.

(ii) It keeps our food fresh.

(iii) It keeps our room cool.

(iv) It helps us solve sums.

(v) It helps wash our clothes.

2. State whether the following statements are true (T) or false (F).

a. Computers work slower than us. ☐

b. A computer is always happy. ☐

c. Computers can store a lot of information. ☐

d. Computers can help add and subtract numbers. ☐

e. Machines make our life easy. ☐

3. Tick (✓) the correct answer.

a. Tick the object that is not a machine.

(i) 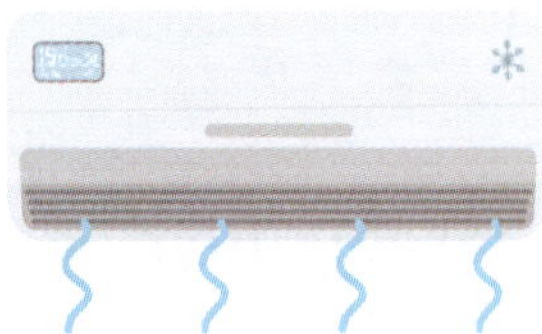

(ii) 

(iii) 

b. Tick the picture that shows a smart machine.

(i) 

(ii) 

(iii) 

c. Tick the machine that runs on electricity.

(i) 

(ii) 

(iii) 

d. Tick the natural thing.

(i) 

(ii) 

(iii) 

4. Look at the following pictures of machines. Rearrange the jumbled words and write their correct names in the blanks given.

a.  RPCUOTME ____________________

b.  KCCLO ____________________

c.  NPTHEELEO ____________________

d.  PAAEENROL ____________________

e.  RXMEI ____________________

5. Complete the following table that shows differences between machines and computers.

electricity many computers

Machines	Computers
a. All machines are not computers.	All __________ are machines.
b. Some machines, for example scissors, do not need ______ to work.	All computers need electricity to work.
c. A machine can perform only one task.	A computer can perform _____ tasks.

6. Colour the picture of computer using colours of your choice.

Lab Activity

Visit the Computer Lab. Do you see any smart machines there? Count and write the number of smart machines you see.

2

Types of Computers

What will I learn?

- What are the different types of computers?
- How to recognize different types of computers in my surroundings?

Think and Discuss

Everyone uses different types of computers. Here are some examples. Tick (✓) the ones that you have seen. Discuss with your teacher and classmates.

1. 

2. 

3. 

4. 

5. 

6. 

Today computers are used everywhere. When someone talks about a computer, we only think of a desktop or a laptop. However, there are different types of computers, which can be divided based on their tasks, size, power and speed.

Here are some commonly used types of computers.

PERSONAL COMPUTER (PC)

A personal computer is a computer made to be used by one person at a time. It is the most common type of computer that we see. At home, a PC is used for playing games, storing photos and surfing the internet. Offices use PCs for sending emails and creating letters, reports and presentations. PCs are also called **microcomputers**.

A personal computer is a computer made to be used by one person at a time.

Desktop Computer

Desktop computer is a type of PC designed to sit on top of a desk or table. It is heavy and works on electricity. Desktops are commonly used in schools and offices and at homes.

Fig. 2.1 *Desktop computer*

A desktop computer is a type of PC that is designed to sit on top of a desk or table.

Knowledge Bytes

Macintosh or Mac is the family of PCs developed by the company, Apple. It was the first PC to have a mouse and interacted with users using graphics. MacBook Pro, MacBook air, and iPad are few examples of Apple machines.

Laptop

A laptop, also known as a notebook/ portable computer, is a type of PC that can be carried around. It is as heavy as 1–3 big bottles of water.

portable: a device that can be easily carried around or moved from one place to another

Laptops operate on battery. They also include a power adapter to recharge the battery.

A laptop is a PC that is designed for travelling.

Fig. 2.2 *Laptop*

Fig. 2.3 *Power adapter*

Tablet

A tablet is a portable PC that uses a touchscreen. Most tablets or tabs are the size of a textbook. They weigh less than a laptop.

Fig. 2.4 *Tablet*

touchscreen: a computer screen that can be used by touching it with a finger or a pen, instead of using a mouse and keyboard

I can tell!

Which of the following devices is not a tablet?

a. Apple iPad ☐ b. Samsung Galaxy Tab ☐

c. Lenovo Smart Tab M10 ☐ d. Kindle ☐

Handheld Computer

A handheld machine or H/PC is a computer that can fit in your hand/pocket. Sometimes, it is also called personal digital assistant (PDA).

Fig. 2.5 *Handheld computer*

Smartphone

A smartphone is a mobile phone that is used to talk to friends and family. When connected to the internet, it can do everything a PC can do.

Fig. 2.6 *Smartphone*

I can tell!

Here are some pictures of different computers. Can you name them using the given words?

Laptop **Tablet** **Mobile phone** **Desktop**

1. 
2. 
3. 
4. 

MINICOMPUTER

A minicomputer is a computer of medium power. It is more powerful than a microcomputer (PC) , but less powerful than a mainframe.

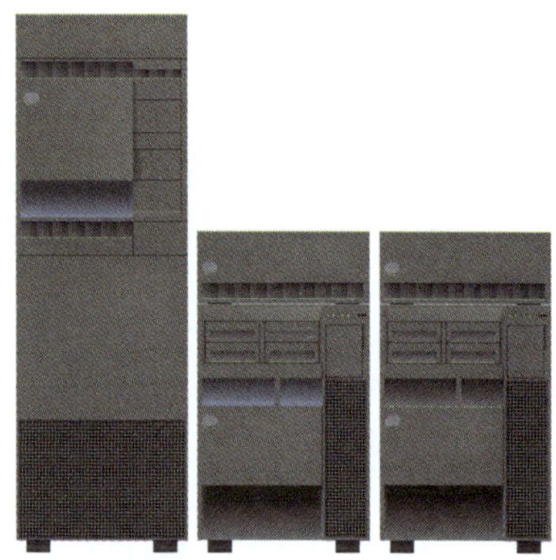

Fig. 2.7 *Minicomputer*

Fig. 2.8 *Mainframe*

MAINFRAME

Mainframes are powerful computers used by large offices only for performing difficult tasks. A mainframe computer is connected to many other computers at a time. It is very fast. The first mainframe computer was made by IBM.

SUPERCOMPUTER

Supercomputers are the Superman of Computers! A supercomputer is big, powerful and very fast, much faster than mainframes. Pratyush is India's fastest supercomputer as of 2020. It is used to study the weather.

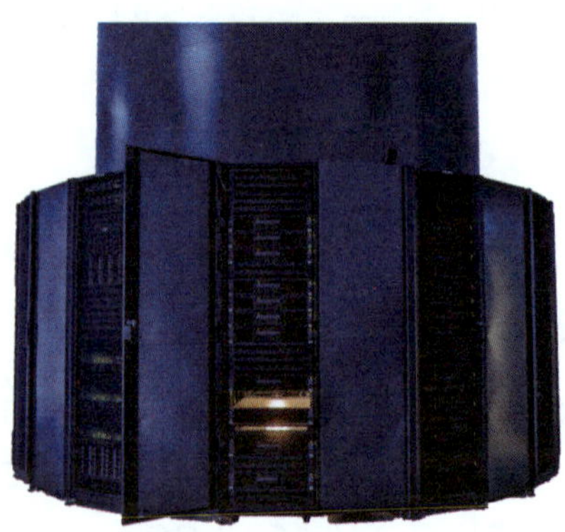

Fig. 2.9 *Supercomputer*

WORKSTATION

A workstation is a personal computer designed for big offices. It is much more powerful than a desktop computer. It is used in certain offices that need to do a lot of work on the computer.

Fig. 2.10 *Workstation*

Fig. 2.11 *Server*

SERVER

A server is a computer that provides data (or information) to many other computers. Big companies use servers to handle all their users and different tasks.

data: pieces of information

WEARABLE COMPUTER

A wearable computer is a small, smart device that can be worn on the body. A smartwatch is the most commonly used wearable computer. Similarly, there are smart goggles, smart rings, smart shoes, and so on.

Fig. 2.12 *Wearable computers*

I can tell!

Observe these computers and mention the objects of similar size.

1. Mainframes — Large fridge
2. Tablets — ____________
3. Laptops — ____________
4. Smartphone — ____________

Desktop

Laptop

Tablet

Smartphone

Supercomputer

Wearable computer

Microcomputer

Handheld computers

Mainframe

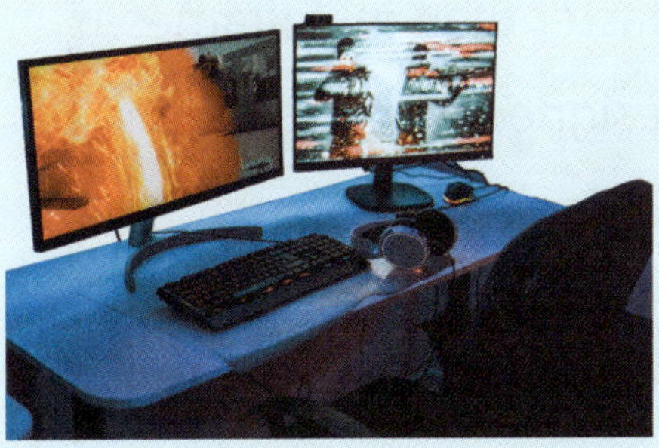

Workstation

Server

What did I learn?

- Different computers are used to perform different tasks.
- Depending on their size, speed and use, computers are divided into multiple types.
- Different types of computers are desktop computer, laptop, tablet, smartphone, mainframe, supercomputer, server, workstation and wearable computer.
- A personal computer is a computer made to be used by one person at a time.
- Desktop computer is a type of PC that is designed to sit on top of a desk or table.
- A laptop, also known as a notebook/portable computer, is a type of PC that can be carried around.
- A tablet is a portable PC that uses a touchscreen.
- A handheld machine or H/PC is a computer that can fit in your hand/pocket.
- A smartphone is the mobile phone used to talk to friends and family.
- A minicomputer is a computer of medium power.
- Mainframes are powerful computers used by large offices only for performing difficult tasks.
- Supercomputers are big, powerful and faster than mainframes.
- A workstation is a personal computer designed for big offices.
- A server is a computer that provides data (or information) to multiple computers.
- A wearable computer is a small, smart device that can be worn on the body.

Exercises

1. State whether the following statements are true (T) or false (F).

a. Mainframes are the most commonly used computers. ☐

b. A supercomputer is bigger than a personal computer. ☐

c. Servers are used in big companies to store information about their customer. ☐

d. Supercomputers and mainframes are used at home. ☐

e. Smart watch is a type of computer. ☐

2. Match the following.

a. Workstation — (i) 

b. PDA — (ii) 

c. Smartphone — (iii) 

d. Wearables — (iv) 

e. Laptop — (v) 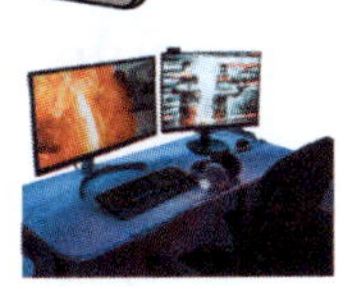

3. Fill in the blanks using the given words.

IBM **wearables** **workstation** **PDA** **Pratyush**

a. Smart rings are types of ________________.

b. ________________ is more powerful than a desktop but less powerful than a supercomputer.

c. ____________________________ is also called handheld computer.

d. The first Mainframe was created by ________________.

e. India's fastest supercomputer is ________________.

4. Tick (✓) the correct answer.

a. Which computer is used in your school computer lab?

(i)  (ii) 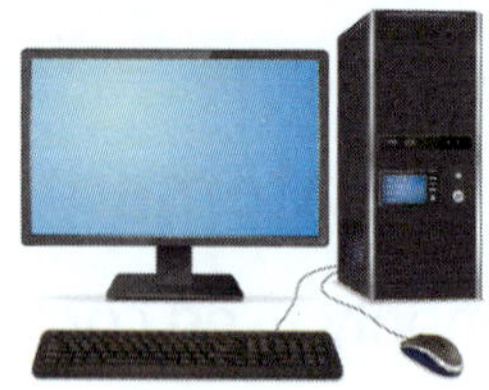 (iii) 

b. Which of the following is not a type of PC?

(i)  (ii)  (iii) 

c. The most powerful computer is:

(i)  (ii)  (iii) 

d. Which of the following computers can be worn on the body?

(i)  (ii)  (iii) 

Lab Activity

Which type of computer do you see in your computer lab? Name its parts.

Think and Answer

1. Look up the meaning of mobile in English dictionary. Why is it called a mobile phone?

 ____

 ____

 ____

2. Gautam loves to listen to music while running. What computer type do you think he should use?

 ____

 ____

 ____

3. Discuss what types of computers you use at home. Draw and colour them on a chart paper.

 ____

 ____

 ____

3 Parts of a Computer

What will I learn?

- What is common between computers and humans?
- What are the different parts of a computer?

Think and Discuss

Look at these pictures. Which parts of the body do we use to do these tasks?

1. Run in the playground

____

2. Smell flowers

____

3. See things around us

____

Different parts of the body are used for different purposes. We have learnt in the last chapter that a *computer is a device that takes instructions from the user, stores and processes it and shows the result*. Just like humans have different body parts, computers have different parts, too. Each part has a function of its own. All the parts work together to make sure the computer runs well.

Four important parts of a computer are:

- Monitor
- CPU
- Keyboard
- Mouse

Fig. 3.1 *Parts of a computer*

MONITOR

A monitor looks like a TV screen. It displays the information we give to the computer. It also shows the result.

It helps us watch pictures and movies on a computer.

Fig. 3.2 *Monitor*

CPU

CPU stands for *Central Processing Unit*. It is the CPU's job to take instructions given by the user and carry them out.

We know in the human body; the brain does the processing. Hence, the CPU is also known as the **brain of the computer**. The more powerful the CPU, the faster the computer.

Fig. 3.3 *CPU*

KEYBOARD

A keyboard is used to give instructions to a computer. It has many buttons called keys. It contains letters, numbers, symbols and some special keys.

Fig. 3.4 *Keyboard*

Knowledge Bytes

Generally, a keyboard has 101 keys.

I can tell!

Look at the keyboard carefully. Why is it called QWERTY keyboard?

Hint: Check the third row on your keyboard.

MOUSE

A mouse helps us to point at different things on the monitor. It is used to give inputs to the computer by taking the cursor to different parts of the screen and clicking.

It is used for selecting, dragging, clicking and opening programs or games.

Today, many computer *mice* are available to be used without a wire as well (wireless mouse).

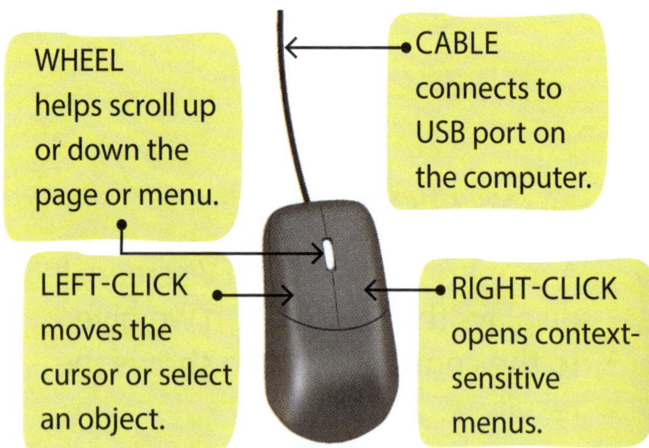

Fig. 3.5 *Computer mouse*

cursor: the moving pointer on the computer that points to the position of the mouse

I am smart!

Laptops have touchpads that can be used to point on the monitor. That is why laptops do not need a mouse.

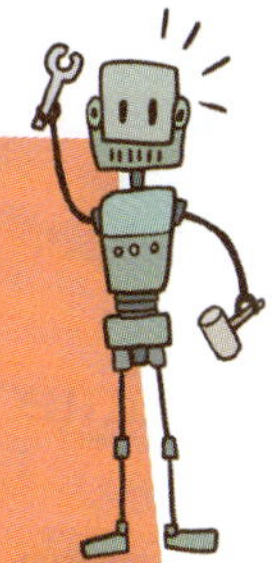

In addition to these, there are other devices that can be connected to the computer for various purposes.

PRINTER

A printer is a device used to take printouts on a piece of paper. It can print pictures and letters.

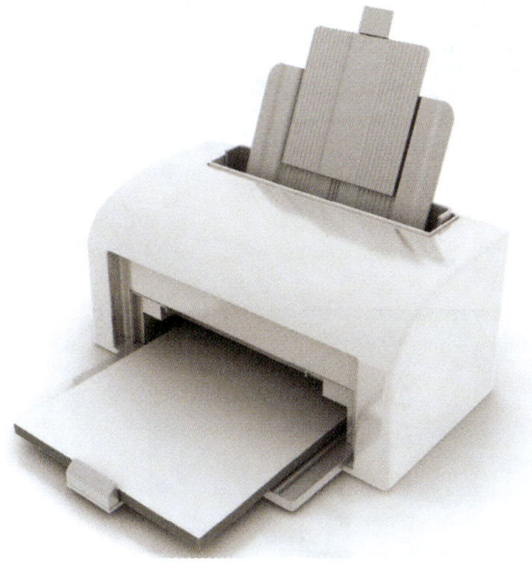

Fig. 3.6 *Printer*

Fig. 3.7 *Speakers*

SPEAKERS

Speakers enable the computer to play sound. We use speakers to listen to songs and audio. Laptops and tablets have in-built speakers in them.

WEBCAM

A webcam is used to make video calls and take pictures. Laptops and tablets already come with a camera in the device. Most desktop monitors do not have an in-built camera and require a separate webcam.

Fig. 3.8 *Webcam*

I can tell!

Name the parts of a computer.

1. 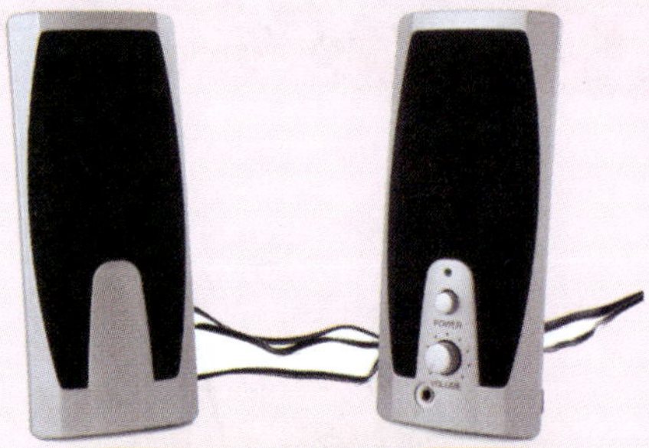

2. 

3. 

4. 

5. 

6. 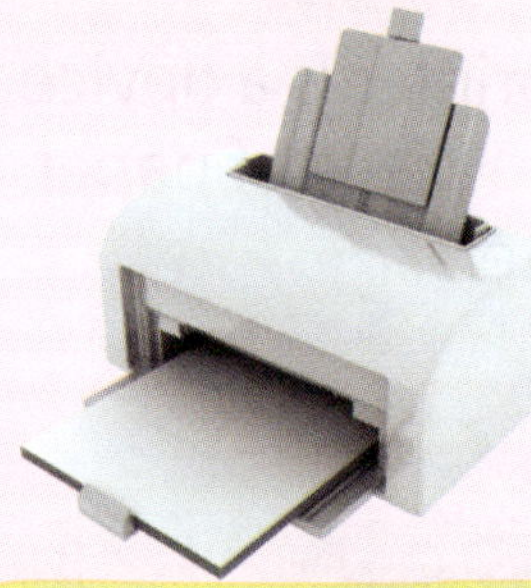

What did I learn?

- The main parts of a computer are the monitor, CPU, keyboard and mouse.
- A monitor, also known as the screen, displays information or results back to the user.
- The CPU is the brain of the computer. It helps run and process everything on the computer.
- A keyboard is used to give instructions to a computer. It has many buttons called keys.
- A mouse is used to give inputs to the computer by taking the cursor to different parts of the screen and clicking.
- Other devices such as printer, speakers and webcam can be connected to the computer to perform different tasks.

Exercises

1. Name the parts of the computer used for the following tasks.

a. Writing stories, letters and emails

____

b. Listening to music

____

c. Playing games

____

2. You already know about various parts of a computer system. Can you mark the following parts on the given picture of laptop?

Monitor **Touchpad** **Keyboard**

3. Colour the following pictures. Also, write their names in the space given.

a.

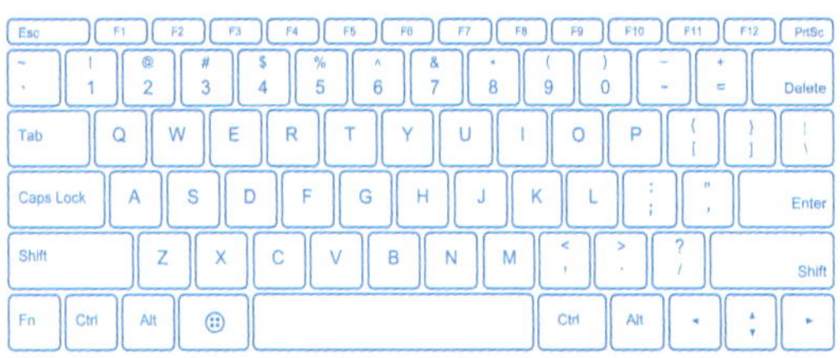

____

b.

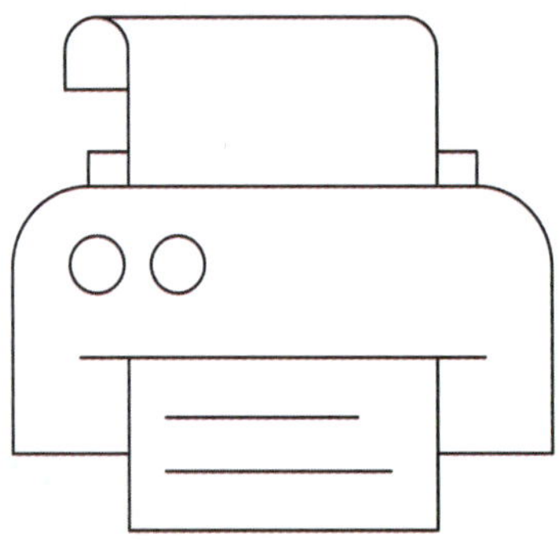

____

c.

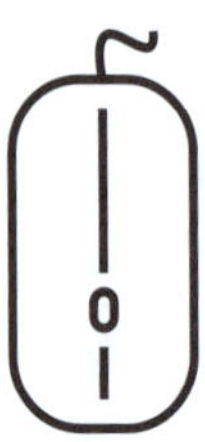

____

d.

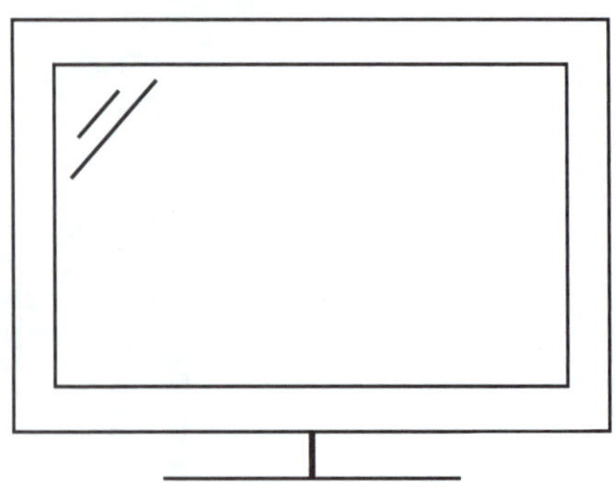

____

4. Rearrange the following jumbled words.

a.

BCWMAE ____________________

b.

UESSMO ____________________

c.

UPC ____________________

d.

RABOKEYD ____________________

e.

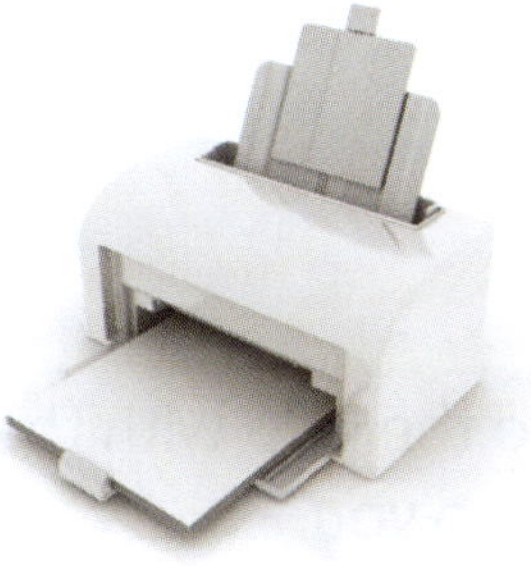

TPERRIN ____________________

5. Fill in the blanks using the given words.

wireless mouse **central processing unit** **symbols** **more** **Speakers**

a. ______________________ are used to listen to songs.

b. The more powerful CPU, the ________________ powerful the computer.

c. The full form of CPU is ______________________________.

d. A mouse used without the wire is known as _______________________.

e. Keyboard contains letters, numbers, ________ and special keys.

6. Match the following.

a. Webcam	(i) Brain of the computer
b. Mouse	(ii) Used to write a letter
c. Keyboard	(iii) Displays the output to the user
d. CPU	(iv) Used to do video calls
e. Monitor	(v) Used to move the cursor on the screen

Group Activity

Go through all the keys on the keyboard and discuss what each of them do with your classmates.

Lab Activity

Monitor, mouse, keyboard, speakers, etc. are connected to the CPU with the help of wires. In the computer lab, ask the teacher to show this to you.

4

Evolution of Communication

What will I learn?

- What is communication?
- How did we communicate in the past?
- How do we communicate now?

Think and Discuss

In your group, show how you will tell your mother you are hungry. Suppose your mother cannot hear what you say. What will you do then?

Now tick (✓) the modes of communication you have used:

1. 
2. 
3. 
4. 
5. 

WHAT IS COMMUNICATION?

As we learned in the activity, we speak and write to share our ideas. This process of sharing thoughts and ideas is called **communication**. When we need to communicate with a person who is far away, we use telephones, computers, etc.

The process of sharing thoughts and ideas is called *communication.*

Today, we can use a computer or telephone to send information or speak to another person. What did people do when there were no computers?

EVOLUTION OF COMMUNICATION

Before Electricity

After Electricity

After Computers

HOW DID WE COMMUNICATE?

Electricity and computers have changed the way we communicate with others. Let us see how.

Before Electricity

Pigeons used to carry letters to people in far-off places. It would take days to send a message. Sometimes, special people called messengers carried letters.

Fig. 4.1 *Modes of communication before electricity*

After Electricity

After we started using electricity, many modes of communication were developed. Examples are fax, telephone, radio and television. Messages were sent immediately. But, it was expensive to share a lot of information. Messages had to be short. A message could be sent to only one person at a time.

messenger: a person who takes messages to someone

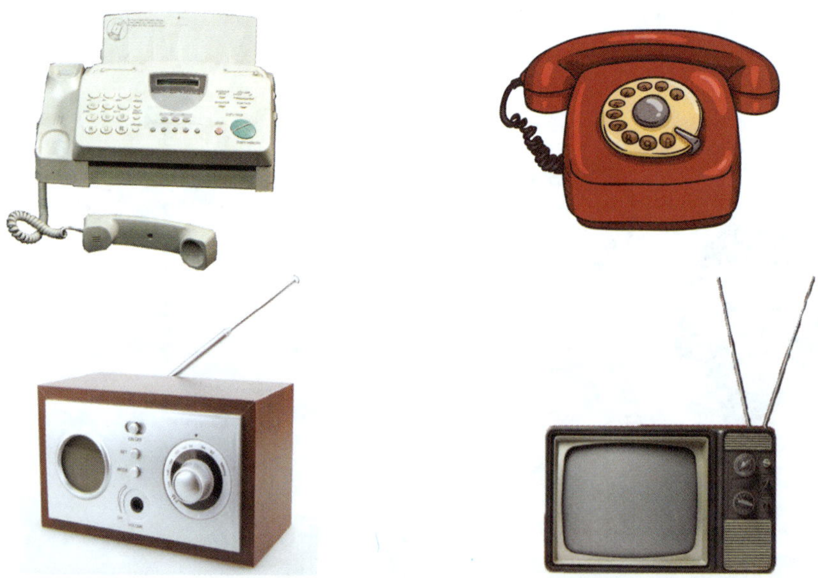

Fig. 4.2 *Modes of communication after electricity*

After Computers

In the last 50 years, computers have become easily available to everyone. We have started using computers for communicating with others. We can share a lot of information with many people using computers. We can send letters on a computer. These letters are called **e-mails**.

Fig. 4.3 *Communication after computers*

The internet, also called the net, connects multiple computers together throughout the world.

With permission, users can get information from any other computer or directly talk to the other person on the computer.

Smartphones or mobile phones

A smartphone is a combination of a computer and a telephone. We can use a smartphone to connect to the internet and send messages to other people. We can also make video calls from anywhere.

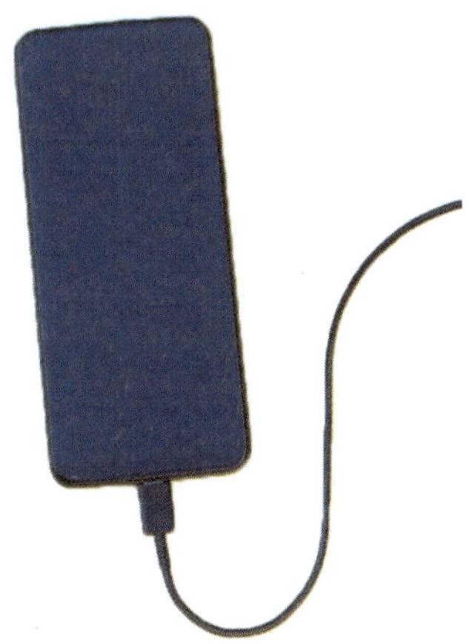

Fig. 4.4 *A smartphone*

I can tell!

Give any three uses of smartphones.

....

....

....

HOW DO WE COMMUNICATE NOW?

Today, we use many methods of communication to share information with people that are far away from us. These methods use a computer and the internet. It takes only a few seconds to send a message.

Also, we can look for any information on the internet.

With the help of a computer or phone connected to the internet, we can read news, find new information, and speak to people in different parts of the world. Here are some common tools we use.

Email

Email stands for electronic mail. It is a letter sent via the internet to the user. To send and receive emails, both the sender and the receiver should have an email address or email id. Gmail, Yahoo mail, and Hotmail are different email providers. Gmail or Google mail is the most widely used email service today.

Fig. 4.5 *Email*

Social Media

Social media is used for sharing messages, pictures and videos with a group of people.

Facebook, Instagram, Snapchat, Twitter and YouTube are a few social media websites/ applications used for different purposes:

- Facebook, Instagram and Snapchat are used to share photos and videos with friends.
- Twitter is mainly used to read and share news.
- YouTube is used specially to create and watch videos.

Knowledge Bytes

Yahoo!, the first email company, was born in 1994.

In the last 200 years, the way we communicate has changed completely. New methods of communication have made the world smaller. We must use it properly and responsibly.

Fig. 4.6 *Various social media applications*

I can tell!

.... is still the most effective form of communication. (Meeting in-person/ Messaging)

Knowledge Bytes

One needs to be at least 13 years old to use social media.

What did I learn?

- The process of sharing thoughts and ideas is called communication.
- Before electricity, pigeons and messengers were used to send and receive messages.
- After electricity, radio, fax, telephone and television were used for communication.
- Computers and the internet changed the way we communicate.
- A smartphone is a combination of a computer and a telephone.
- Now, we can communicate with others using email and social media.

Exercises

1. Tick (✓) the correct answer.

a. Which of the following is a social media platform?

(i) Google ☐ (ii) YouTube ☐ (iii) Wikipedia ☐

b. Which of these methods of communication is used today?

(i) Telegram ☐ (ii) Smoke signals ☐ (iii) Email ☐

c. Which of these is not a form of communication?

(i) Social media ☐ (ii) Email ☐ (iii) Sleeping ☐

d. Which of these can be used to make video calls?

(i) Laptop ☐ (ii) Smartphone ☐ (iii) Both (i) and (ii) ☐

e. What is the full form of email?

(i) Electronic mail ☐ (ii) Elementary mail ☐ (iii) Elected mail ☐

f. Which of the following modes of communication use electricity?

(i) Pigeons ☐ (ii) Messengers ☐ (iii) Smartphones ☐

g. Which of the following is not possible while using a radio?

(i) Hear the news ☐ (ii) Listen to songs ☐ (iii) See videos ☐

2. Match the following.

a.	Letter	(i)	Used to watch tv shows and movies
b.	YouTube	(ii)	Handwritten
c.	Email	(iii)	Used to speak to a person far away from us
d.	Pigeon	(iv)	Used to send messages over long distances in the past
e.	Telephone	(v)	Used to share video content to the world.
f.	Television	(vi)	Requires an email address

3. Rearrange the following jumbled words.

a.  MUPCOERT ____________________

b.  BKCOOEAF ____________________

c.  UOBETUY ____________________

d.  ILEMA ____________________

e.  IDORA ____________________

4. Fill in the blanks using the given words.

smartphones **videos** **one-way** **letter** **social media**

a. Television is a ___________ communication.

b. Most phones used today are ________________.

c. Email is an electronic form of a ______________.

d. YouTube is used to watch ________________.

e. Facebook and Instagram are examples of ___________ __________ platforms.

5. We have learned that computers have changed the way we communicate with others. What could be the next stage in communication? Imagine and draw what it could be.

6. Rearrange the different modes of communication in the order of when they came first.

Smartphones   Pigeon   Internet   Radio   Telephone   TV   Emails   Telegrams   Messengers

____

____

____

7. Find and circle the hidden modes of communication in this picture.

5 Fun with Tux Paint

What will I learn?

- What is Tux Paint?
- How can I use various Tux Paint tools to draw on a computer?

Think and Discuss

Draw the following shapes and colour them.

Paper, pencil, crayons, etc. are used to make drawings in real life. Similarly as Tux Paint helps us make drawings on a computer. Let us see how.

Similar to drawing on a notebook, we can use a computer to draw and colour pictures.

In this chapter, we will learn how we can use **Tux Paint** for creating drawing on a computer .

WHAT IS TUX PAINT?

Tux Paint is a free, drawing program on the computer, specially made for children. It is easy to use and is used in schools around the world. It also has fun sound effects.

HOW TO OPEN TUX PAINT?

The steps to open Tux Paint on a computer are given below:

1. Click on the **Start** button on the bottom-left of the screen.
2. Select the **Tux Paint** folder.
3. Click on the **Tux Paint (Windowed)** option (Fig. 5.1).

> **Knowledge Bytes**
>
> Tux is a penguin who helps children when they get stuck.

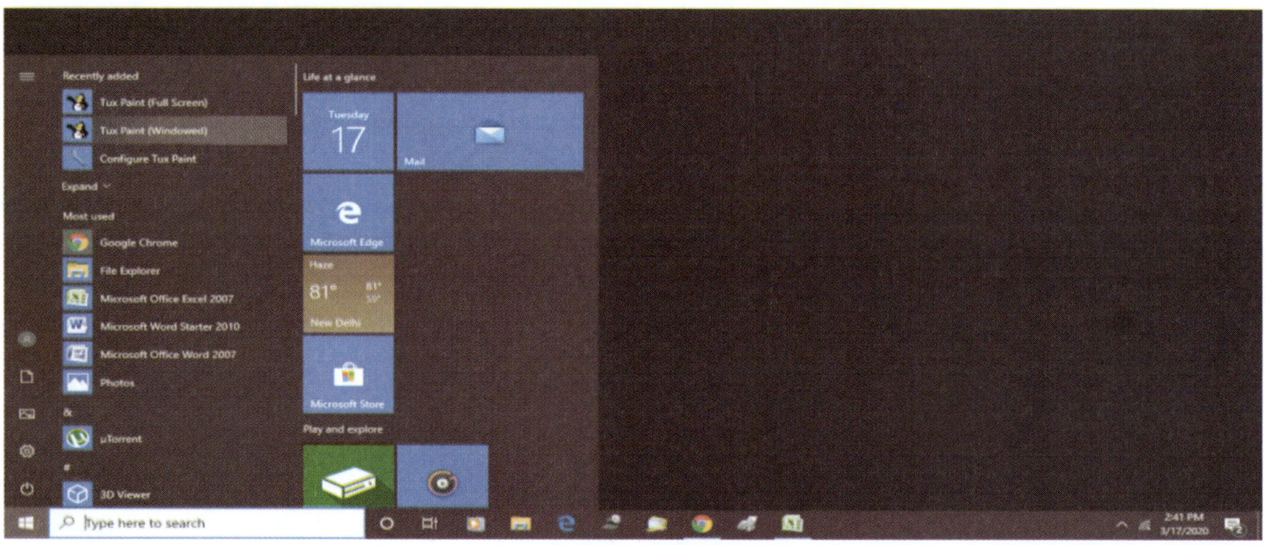

Fig. 5.1 *Opening Tux Paint*

Alternatively, double-click on the Tux Paint icon present on the desktop of the computer.

I can do!

After selecting the Tux Paint folder, we click on the Tux Paint (Windowed) option. Now click on the Tux Paint (Full Screen) option. What happens? Write it down here.

....

....

Once Tux Paint is launched, we first see the welcome screen (Fig. 5.2). Then, we see the home screen of the Tux Paint program (Fig. 5.3).

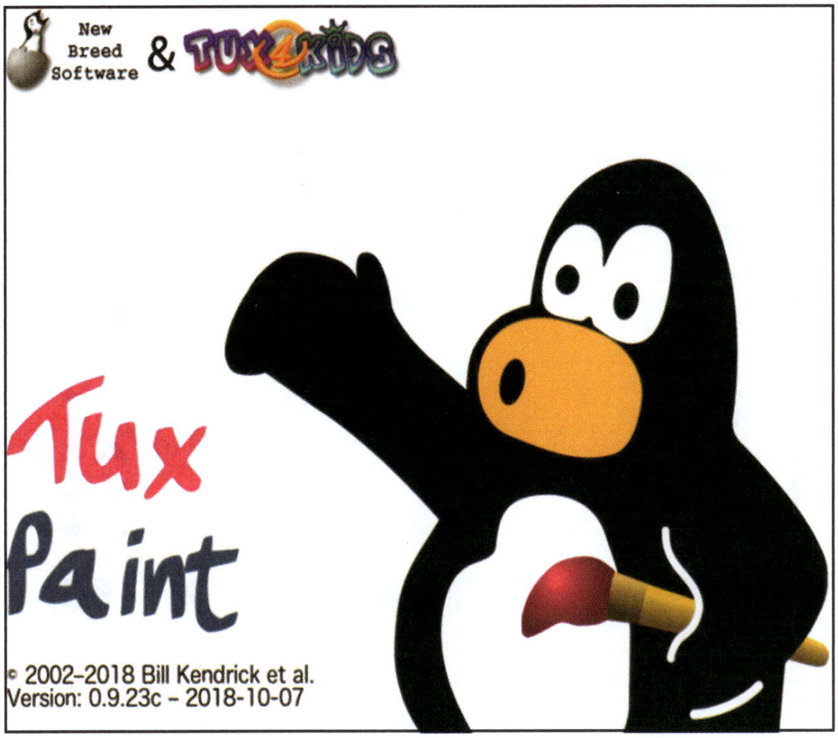

Fig. 5.2 *Welcome screen of Tux Paint*

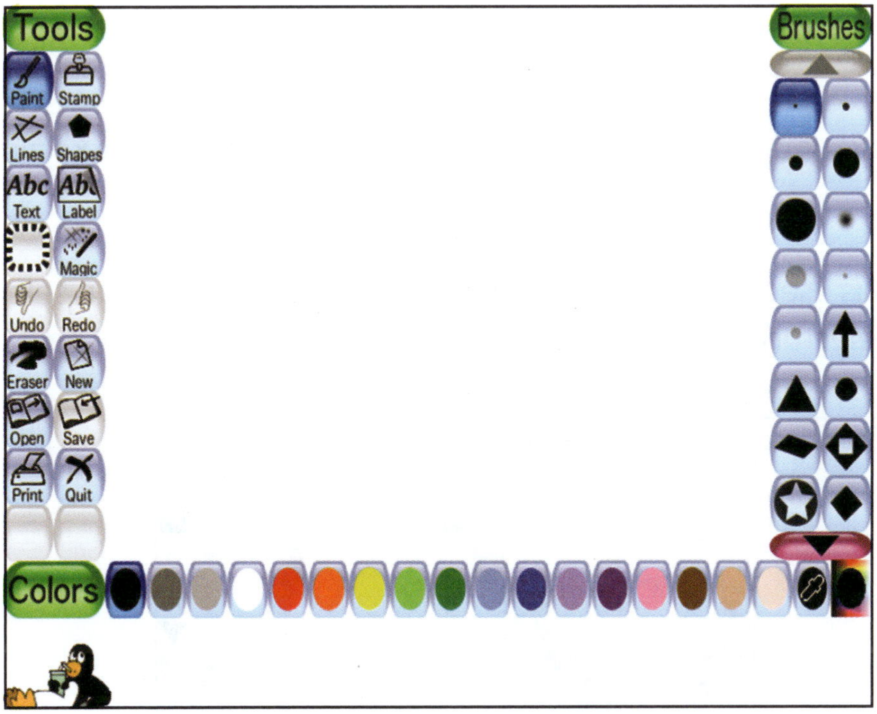

Fig. 5.3 *Home screen of Tux Paint*

PARTS OF THE TUX PAINT WINDOW

The home screen of Tux Paint is divided into five parts, as shown in Fig. 5.4.

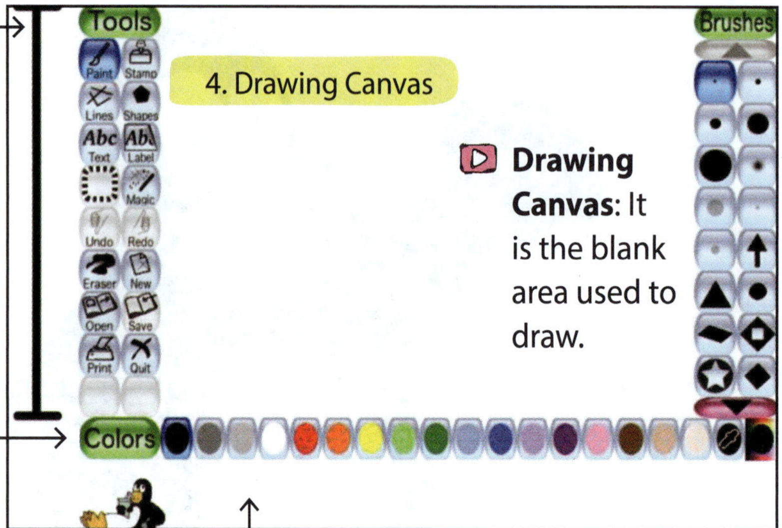

Toolbar: It contains the drawing and editing tools.

Colors: It is used to choose different colours to make a drawing.

Drawing Canvas: It is the blank area used to draw.

Help Area: It shows suggestions related to the selected tool.

Selector: It shows various options related to the tools selected in the Toolbar. For example, for the Paint tool, the selector shows various Brushes.

Fig. 5.4 *Parts of Tux Paint window*

TOOLBAR

Let us learn and understand some of the tools available in the Tux Paint Toolbar.

Paint

The Paint tool is used to make freehand drawing (Fig. 5.5). We can select any brush (from Selector) and colour (from Colors) to make our drawing.

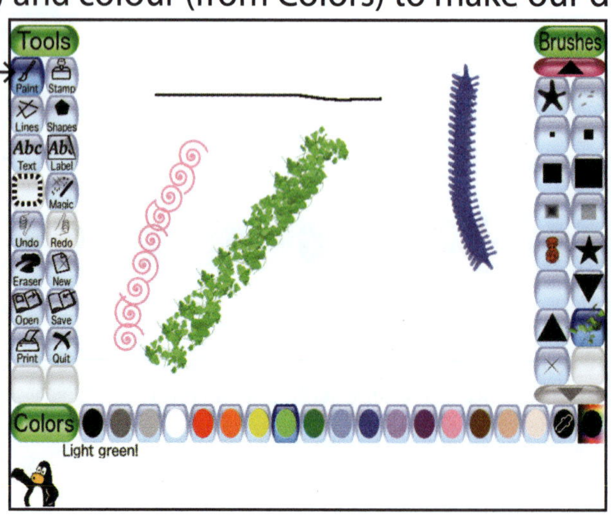

Fig. 5.5 *Using the Paint tool*

Stamp

Stamp is a fun option, which stamps the image of Tux in our drawing. For selecting a stamp, follow the steps given below:

1. Click on the **Stamp** tool.
2. Select a stamp from the available Stamps on the right (Fig. 5.6).
3. Click on the drawing area where the stamp needs to appear.

I am smart!

We can download and add additional stamps from the official website of Tux Paint: http://www.tuxpaint.org/download/windows/

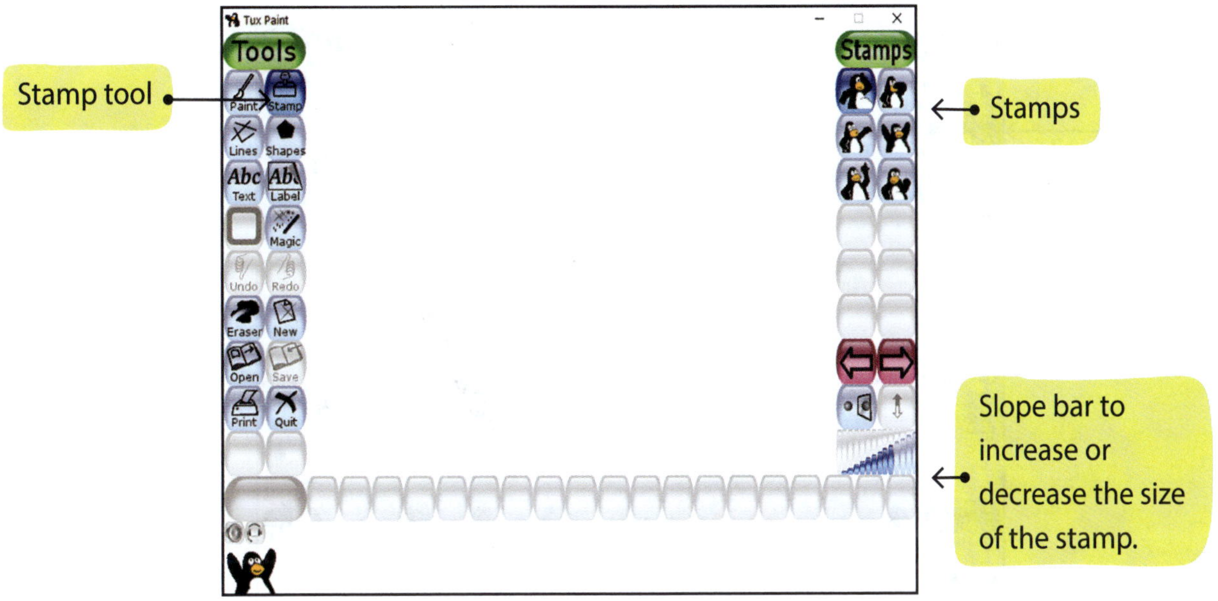

Fig. 5.6 *Using the Stamp tool*

I can do!

Explore the option in Fig. 5.6. Write down what it does.

....

....

....

Lines

The **Lines** tool lets us draw straight lines. When we select this tool, the Selector shows us various options of brushes to choose from.

For drawing a line, follow the steps given below:

1. Click on the **Lines** tool.
2. Select a brush from the available Brushes on the right.
3. Click and hold the mouse button and drag it to the length you want. Release the mouse button when you are done.

Figure 5.7 shows various lines drawn using this tool.

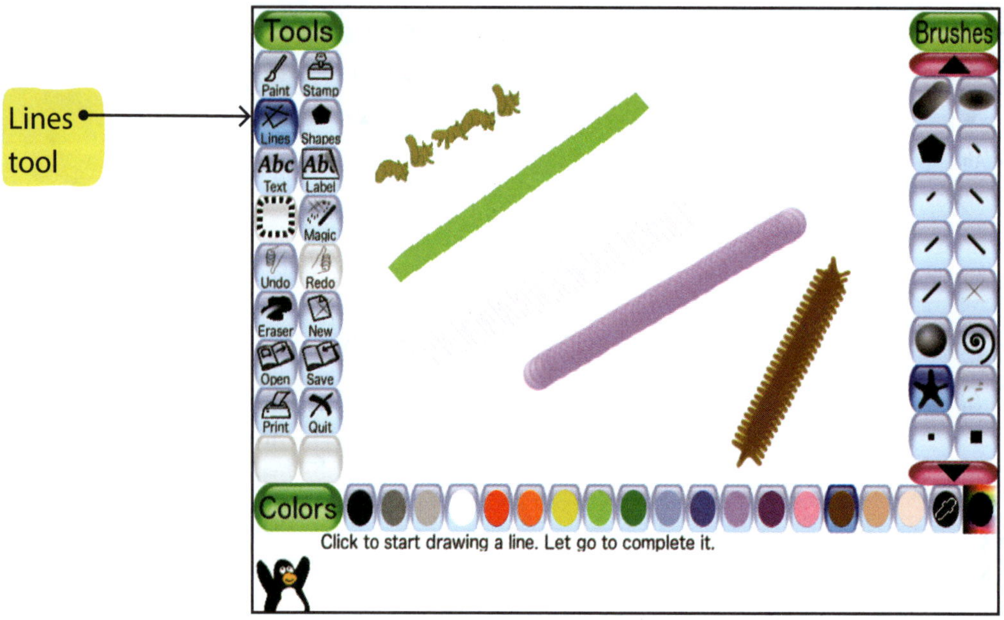

Fig. 5.7 *Using the Lines tool*

I can tell!

Tick (✓) the correct answer.

a. Which tool will you use to make a freehand drawing?

(i) Paint tool ☐ (ii) Line tool ☐

b. Which tool will you use to draw straight lines?

(i) Paint tool ☐ (ii) Line tool ☐

Shapes

The **Shapes** tool is used to draw different shapes. To add shapes to the drawing, follow the steps given below:

1. Click on the **Shapes** tool.
2. Select any shape from the Shapes given on the right.
3. Click and hold the mouse button and drag it to the size you want. Release the mouse button when you are done.

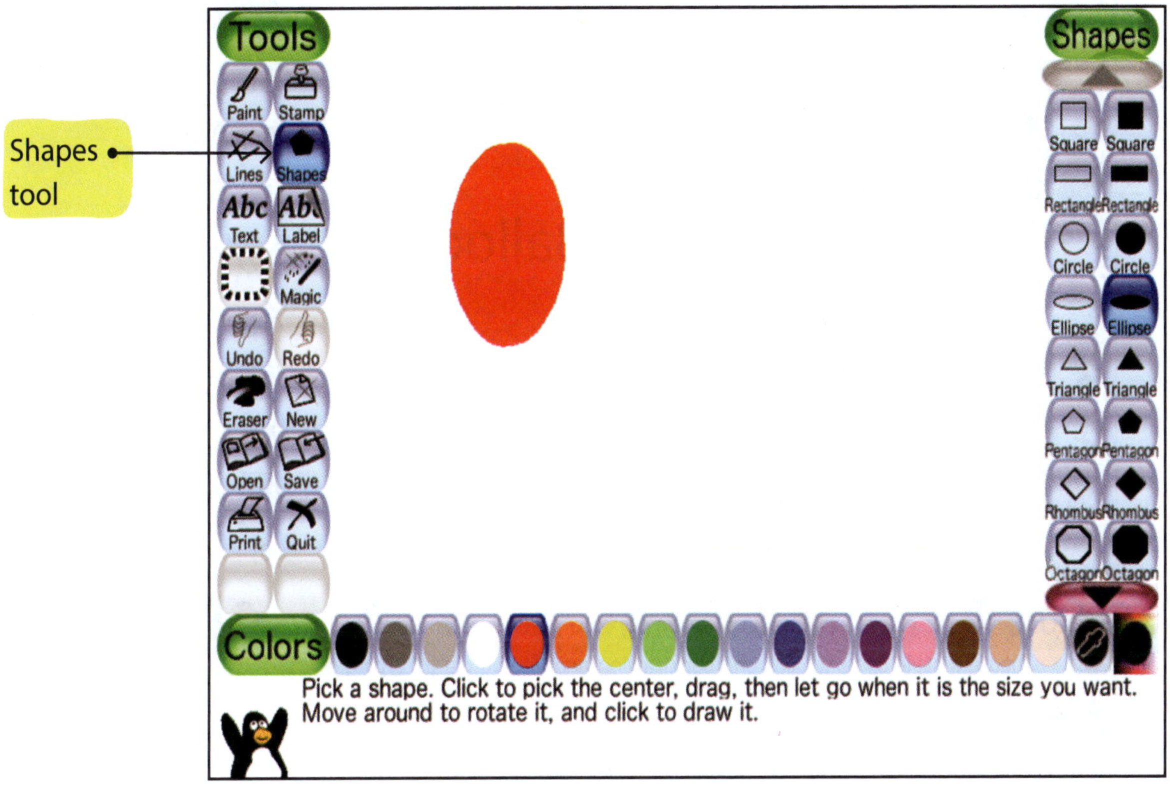

Fig. 5.8 *Using the Shapes tool*

I can do!

The option [color-picker icon] on the bottom-right is known as the color-picker. Click on this option and find out what it does. Write down what you see.

....

....

....

Text

The **Text** tool is used to write next to the drawing or on the drawing. Follow these steps to add text in a drawing:

1. Click on the **Text** tool from the toolbar. A list of **Letters** appears on the right. Select the style from here.
2. Click on the place in the drawing area where you want your text to appear. Now start typing the text (Fig. 5.9).

Fig. 5.9 *Using the Text tool*

I can do!

The up and down arrows appear with the Text tool. Click on them and find out what happens. Write down what you see.

....

....

Undo  and Redo 

If we do not like something we drew, or want to go back to our last state, we use the **Undo** option. To use Undo, simply click on the option. Click the **Redo** button to redo the drawing action we just cancelled with the Undo button.

I am smart!

We can use Undo and Redo buttons more than once.

Eraser

It is used to erase any part of a drawing. The Eraser comes in various sizes and shapes. To use the eraser, follow the steps given below:

1. Click on the **Eraser** from the toolbar.
2. Select the shape and the size of the **Eraser** from the right.
3. Click and drag the mouse over the part of the drawing you want to erase.

Fig. 5.10 *Using the Eraser tool*

New

To make a new drawing, use the **New** option. There are some drawings already saved on top for you to colour or change.

Fig. 5.11 *Using the New option*

We can explore more background options by clicking on the arrow (Fig. 5.12).

Fig. 5.12 *More backgrounds*

Figure 5.13 shows a hat background. We can draw around this background using the various Tools.

Fig. 5.13 *Hat background selected*

Remember that background drawings cannot be erased once selected.

Save

The **Save** option saves our drawing in Tux Paint. When we click on this option, the Help Area shows a message 'Your image has been saved!'.

Fig. 5.14 *Saved drawing*

Open

To open a saved drawing, simply click on the **Open** option. The list of saved drawings is displayed. To go back to the drawing, click on the 

button.

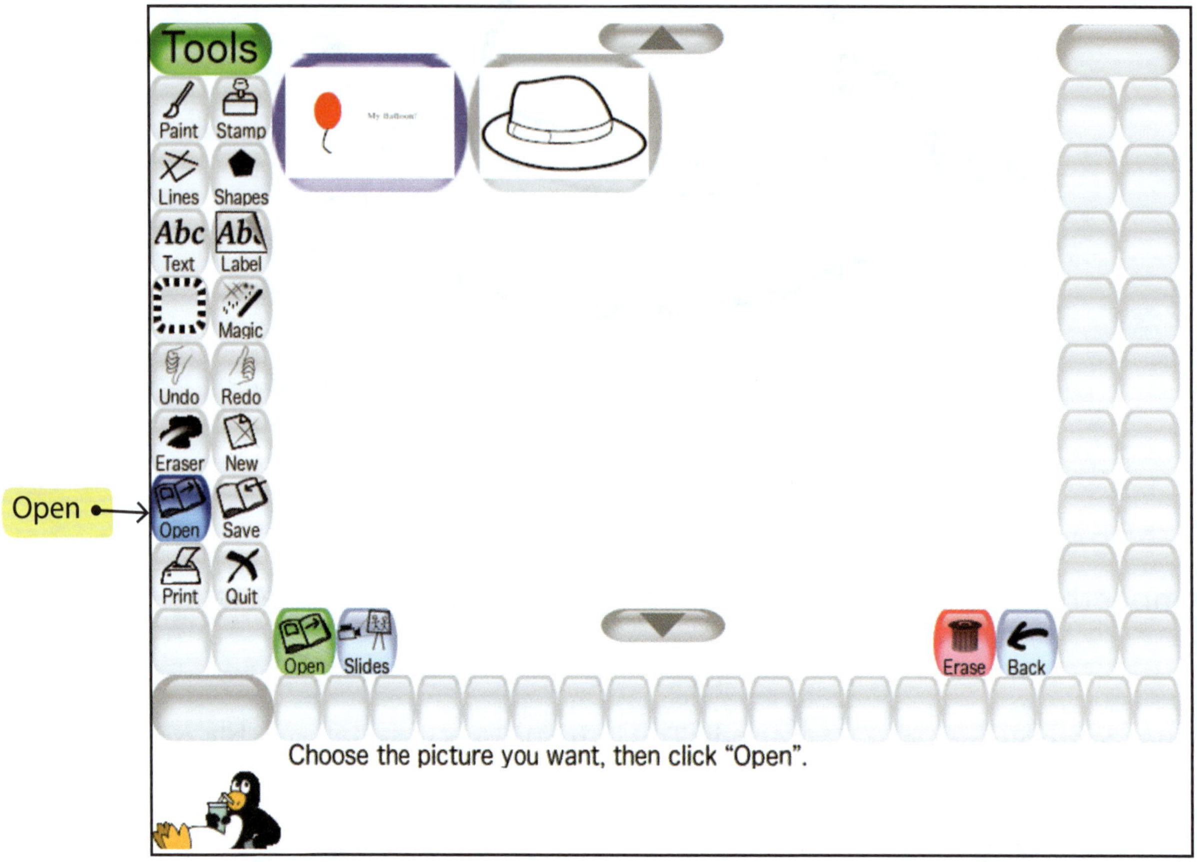

Fig. 5.15 *Using the Open option*

I can do!

Explore the 

button and write down what it does.

....

....

....

Print 

The printer is an output device. When connected to the computer, this option prints a drawing on paper.

Quit

It is used to close the Tux Paint application. When we click on this button, it shows us a message, as shown in Fig. 5.16.

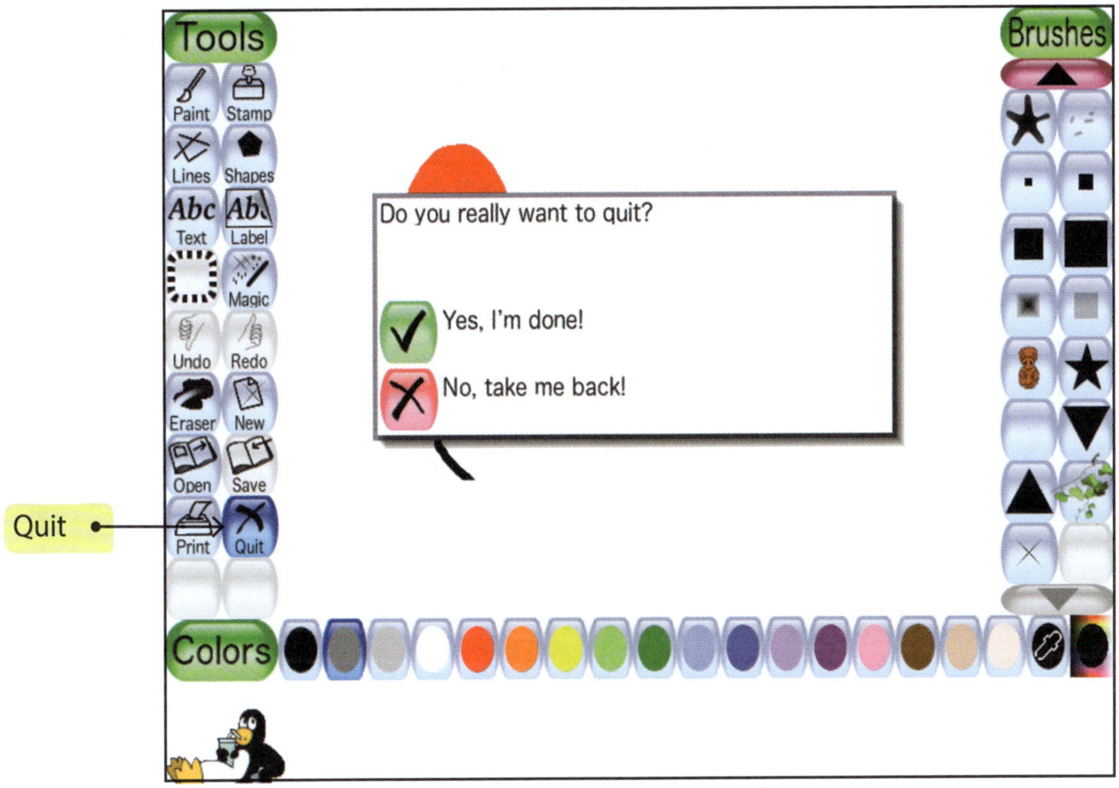

Fig. 5.16 *Quitting Tux Paint*

I can do!

Explore the following options in Tux Paint. Write down what they do.

a.  ....

....

b.  ....

....

What did I learn?

- Tux Paint is a free, drawing software application on the computer, specially for children, used to draw and colour.
- It has special sound effects and Tux the penguin to help when we are stuck.
- The Tux Paint window is divided into five parts: Toolbar, Drawing Canvas, Colors, Selector and Help Area.
- The Toolbar has many options to help us draw. Paint, Lines, Shapes and Text are some of the options.
- The Selector shows the various options available for the selected Tool option. For the Text tool, the Selector shows the letters in many styles.
- The Undo, Redo and Erase options can be used to make changes to drawings.
- The Save option is used to save the drawing in the computer.
- The New and Open options can be used to make new drawings and open saved drawings.
- The Quit option is used to close Tux Paint.

Exercises

1. Fill in the blanks using the given words.

New **Brushes** **Paint** **Tux** **Open**

a. _________ is the name of the Penguin that helps in Tux Paint.

b. The Paint tool has many _________ to choose from.

c. Tux Paint can be used to draw and _________.

d. We can open saved drawings with the help of _________.

e. To make a new drawing, _________ option is used.

2. Match the following.

a. 

(i) 

b. 

\+ 

(ii) 

c. 

\+ 

(iii) 

d. 

(iv) 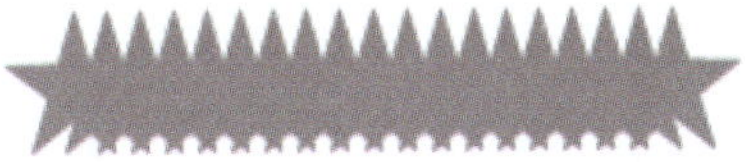

3. State whether the following statements are true (T) or false (F).

a. Tux Paint is used by children. ☐

b. Tux Paint can be used to make videos. ☐

c. Lines and Shapes tools have the Brushes option. ☐

d. Tux Paint does not have sound effects. ☐

e. Drawings cannot be erased in Tux Paint. ☐

4. Search the following words in the word grid given below.

Brushes **Shapes** **Save** **Paint** **Lines** **Print** **Quit**

S	B	X	K	B	L
D	R	C	L	S	I
Q	U	V	P	A	N
W	S	P	Z	V	E
S	H	A	P	E	S
K	E	I	R	J	K
L	S	N	I	H	L
P	K	T	N	F	P
Q	U	I	T	T	Y

Lab Activity

1. Draw the following shapes using the colours of your choice using Tux Paint.

   - Square
   - Circle
   - Two lines
   - A circle and a line
   - A circle inside a triangle

2. Draw the following on Tux Paint.

   - Ball
   - Book
   - Pencil
   - Cat

3. Use the following shapes to draw a cat using Tux Paint tools.

   - Circle
   - Oval
   - Triangle
   - Lines

4. Create a drawing using the various Brushes in the Line and Paint options.

Worksheet 1

1. Tick (✓) the correct answer.

a. Tick the part of the computer that is used to point on the screen.

(i) 

(ii) 

(iii) 

b. Tick the natural thing.

(i) 

(ii) 

(iii) 

c. Tick the part of the computer used to type on a computer.

(i) 

(ii) 

(iii) 

d. Tick the computer that is used in schools.

(i) 

(ii) 

(iii) 

e. Tick the thing that is not a machine.

(i) 

(ii) 

(iii) 

2. Match the following.

a. 

b. 

c. 

d. 

e. 

(i) A type of personal computer that cannot be moved

(ii) Gives instructions to the computer using keys

(iii) Displays information back to the user

(iv) Small computers worn by people

(v) Points at different things on the monitor

3. Fill in the blanks using the given words.

server **handheld** **mouse** **humans** **machine**

a. The things made by ________ are called human-made things.

b. A ________ is a computer that provides data to multiple other computers.

c. A computer is a ________ that takes instructions from the user, stores it and processes it to show results.

d. A ________ is used to open a program on a computer.

e. A smartphone is a type of ________ computers.

4. State whether the following statements are true (T) or false (F).

a. A computer gets tired easily. ☐

b. A calculator is a smart machine. ☐

c. The CPU is called the brain of the computer. ☐

d. A desktop computer is an example of a minicomputer. ☐

e. All parts of the computer are connected to the monitor. ☐

5. Colour the correct option to answer the following questions.

a. Nilima wants to print a document from the computer so she can show it to her class the next day. Which output device does she need to print the pictures from the computer on a paper?

(i) 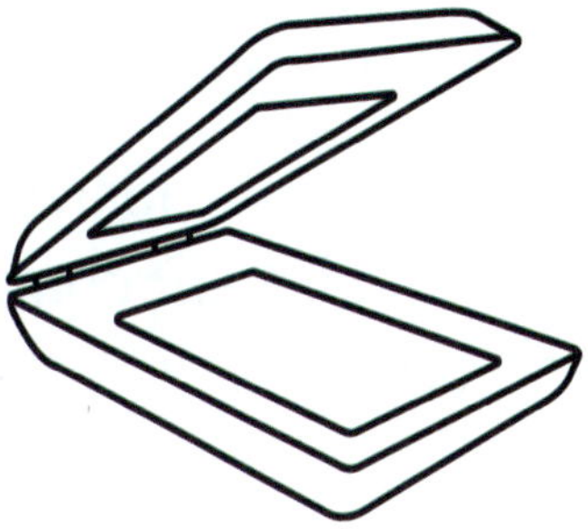

(ii) 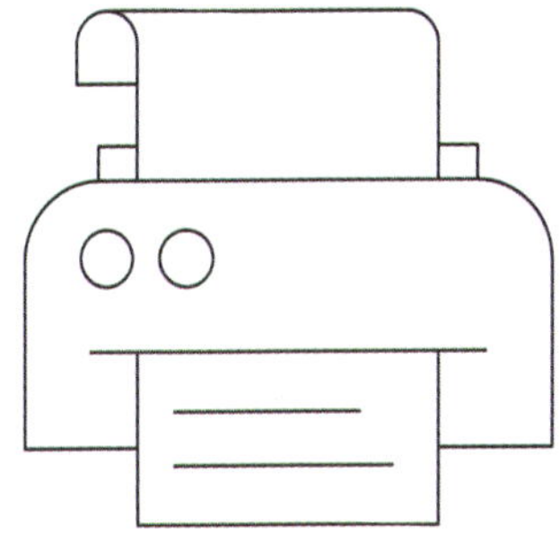

b. Ishan wants to make a video call to his friend in the USA. Which additional device will he have to use to see his friend?

(i) 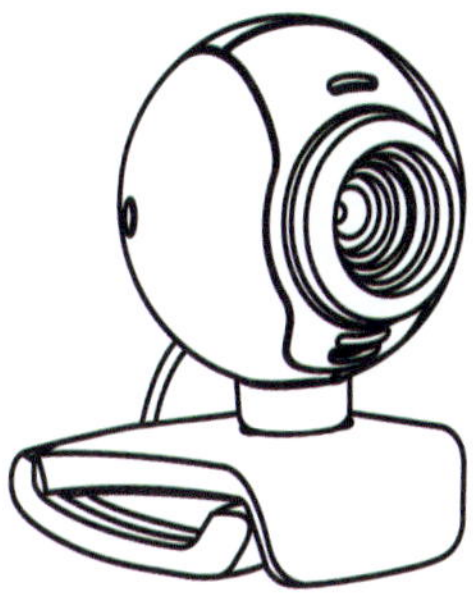

(ii) 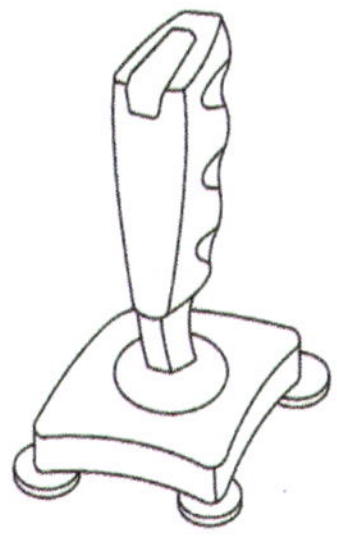

c. Smriti loves to go to many places for work. Which type of computer should she buy so she can carry it around and work?

(i) 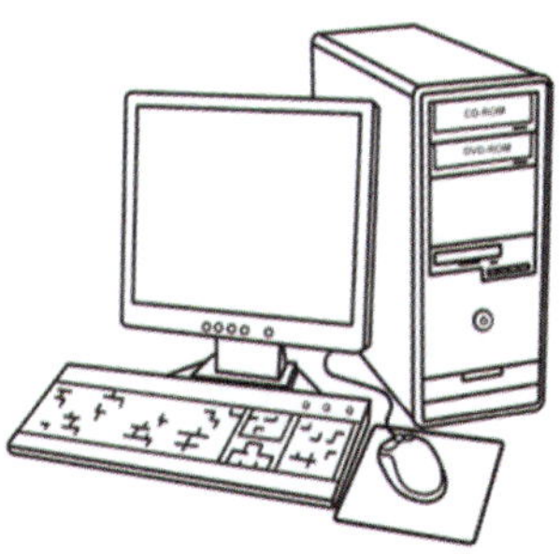

(ii) 

d. Gaurav is playing a video game on his computer. Which additional device does he need to move the character in any direction on the screen?

(i) 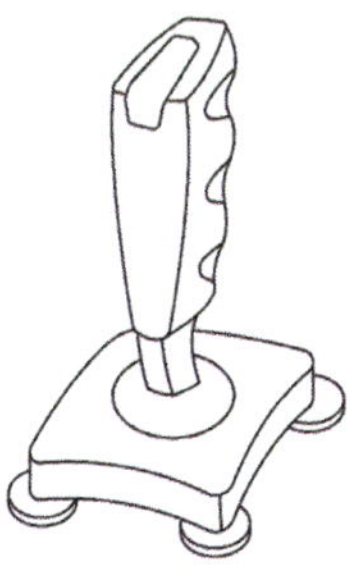

(ii) 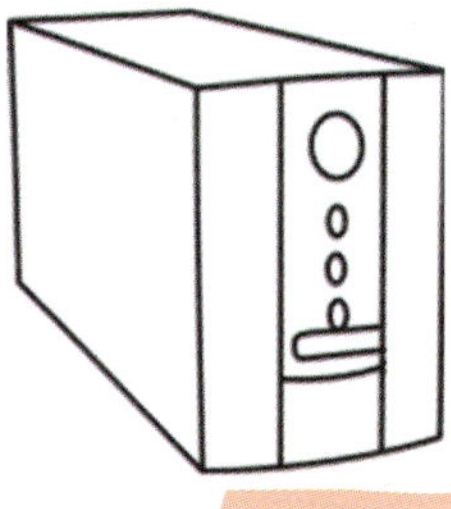

Projects

1. When you travel from home to school, what machines and natural things do you come across? Draw and name three of each.
2. What type of computer have your seen in the lab? Draw and colour it.
3. Write down all kinds of computers you have seen at home and in the school. On a chart paper, draw and colour them. Use different colours for different types of computers. Write what each computer is used for.

Worksheet 2

1. Tick (✓) the correct answer.

a. Tick the mode of communication that does not use electricity.

(i) 

(ii) 

(iii) 

b. Tick the program that is used to make drawings in a computer.

(i) 

(ii) 

(iii) 

c. Tick the mode of communication that can be used with the internet.

(i) 

(ii) 

(iii) 

d. Tick the tool that is used to add text to a drawing in Tux Paint.

(i) 

(ii) 

(iii) 

e. Tick the options we see in the Selector when the Lines tool is selected.

(i)

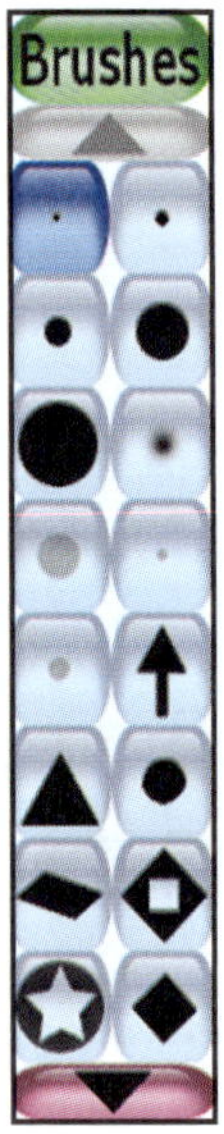

(ii)

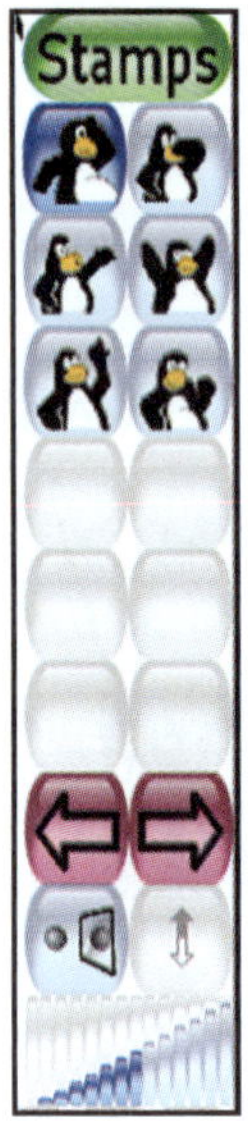

(iii)

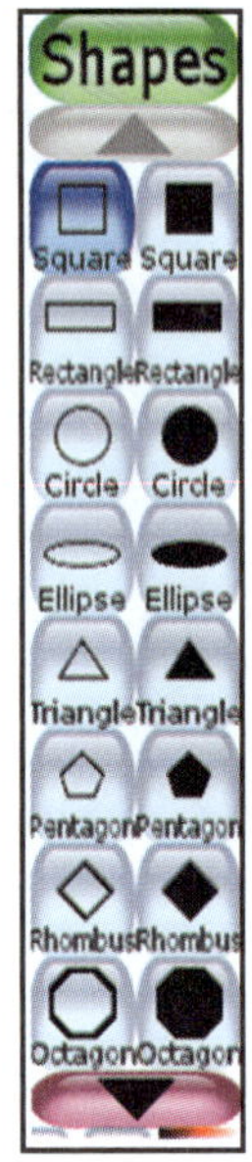

2. Fill in the blanks using the correct option.

a. The Text tool is used for ____________ text in the Tux Paint. (typing/printing)

b. ____________ is not possible by using a radio. (Listening to songs/Watching videos)

c. ____________ tool is used to add images of Tux in our drawings. (Stamp/Bucket)

d. The process of sharing thoughts and ideas is called ____________. (processing/ communication)

e. ____________ is a mode of communication that uses electricity. (Pigeon/ Smartphone)

3. State whether the following statements are true (T) or false (F).

a. Tux Paint is a very costly software application. ☐

b. A smartphone is a combination of a computer and a telephone. ☐

c. We cannot print drawings created using Tux Paint. ☐

d. Email is a letter sent via the internet to the user. ☐

e. We use pigeons to send letters to people in far-off places. ☐

4. Find the following words in the grid given below.

Lines **Computer** **Tux** **Shapes** **Mobile** **Email**

E	M	O	S	I	L	L	M
M	E	A	H	Z	S	I	O
A	M	E	A	T	T	N	U
C	O	M	P	U	T	E	R
L	B	A	E	X	L	S	E
T	I	I	S	N	O	T	E
W	L	L	E	N	E	C	S
X	E	B	L	E	T	R	K

5. Match the following.

a.  (i) Shapes

b.  (ii) Lines

c.  (iii) Stamp

d.  (iv) Eraser

e.  (v) Paint

Projects

a. Draw a scenery using Tux Paint.

b. From magazines, cut out pictures of five modes of communication. Paste them on a chart paper. Write one sentence about each. Show your project to your class. Tell them about your favourite mode of communication.

Computer Manners

Always follow the instructions of your computer teacher in the lab.

1. Do not pull or push the keyboard too hard. It may damage the wires.	2. Do not use a wet cloth to clean the computer. It may damage its parts.

✗	✗
3. Do not eat or drink anything while using the computer. Food or drinks may spill on it.	4. Keep the computer room clean. Dust may damage the computer parts.

✗	✓

5. Do not sit too close to the computer screen. It may harm your eyes.	6. Always use a mouse pad for the mouse.

✗	✓
7. Do not take a magnet near a computer.	8. Do not push the computer table. Some part may fall and get damaged.

✗	✗

About the Authors

Sneha Krishnan and **Manasi Kashikar**, techies at heart, bond over their love of coding. They are co-founders of the company *MindChamp* where they teach coding to school students using fun, activity-based learning. They both love to teach students and that reflects in their work. Together with a team of educators, they have taught thousands of students to create computer games and websites. They want to make coding accessible to young students as well, so they are better equipped for the future.